ANIMAL RIVALS

Shark
vs.
Killer Whale

Isabel Thomas

raintree
a Capstone company — publishers for children

Raintree is an imprint of Capstone Global Library Limited, a company incorporated in England and Wales having its registered office at 264 Banbury Road, Oxford, OX2 7DY – Registered company number: 6695582

www.raintree.co.uk
myorders@raintree.co.uk

Edited by Penny McLoughlin
Designed by Steve Mead
Picture research by Svetlana Zhurkin
Production by Katy LaVigne
Printed and bound in China

ISBN 978 1 474 74450 8
21 20 19 18 17
10 9 8 7 6 5 4 3 2 1

British Library Cataloguing in Publication Data
A full catalogue record for this book is available from the British Library.

Acknowledgements
We would like to thank the following for permission to reproduce photographs: Getty Images: Jeff Rotman, 22 (bottom right); iStockphoto: DaveRig, 9, Elizabeth Hoffmann, 20, Grafissimo, 17, Lazareva, 19; Minden Pictures: Doug Perrine, 11, Hiroya Minakuch, 7; National Geographic Creative: Paul Nicklen, 15; Shutterstock: aarrows (silhouette), 6, 7, Alessandro De Maddalena, 12, 22 (top right), Alexius Sutandio, 4, Arend van der Walt, 10, 22 (middle left), David Pruter, cover (right), Martin Prochazkacz, 16, Mike Price, 5, 21, Monika Wieland, back cover (right), 13, nitrogenic, 14, 22 (bottom left), pashabo (texture), cover and throughout, Sergey Uryadnikov, 18, VisionDive, cover (left), wildestanimal, back cover (left), 6, 8, 22 (top left, middle right)

Every effort has been made to contact copyright holders of material reproduced in this book. Any omissions will be rectified in subsequent printings if notice is given to the publisher.

All the Internet addresses (URLs) given in this book were valid at the time of going to press. However, due to the dynamic nature of the Internet, some addresses may have changed, or sites may have changed or ceased to exist since publication. While the author and publisher regret any inconvenience this may cause readers, no responsibility for any such changes can be accepted by either the author or the publisher.

Some words are shown in bold, **like this**.
You can find them in the glossary on page 22.

Contents

Meet the animals

What has a back **fin** and razor-sharp teeth?

It's the **great white shark**.

What's huge with black and white skin?

It's the
killer whale, also
called an orca.

Would a shark or a killer whale win in
a fight?
Let's find out!

Size

A shark is so huge it can eat almost anything, from small squid to big seals. Once a shark was caught with two whole sea lions in its stomach.

This is how big a shark is next to a human.

This is how big a killer whale is next to a human.

Killer whales are even bigger than sharks. A male killer whale can weigh the same as two elephants. A newborn baby killer whale is as long as a car!

Speed

A shark is a swimming machine. Its powerful body is packed with **muscles**, but most of the time it moves slowly to save energy.

The killer whale's smooth body moves through the water easily. It can swim up to six times faster when chasing **prey**.

Skin colour

Clever colouring helps a shark stay out of sight as it sneaks up on its **prey**. When seen from above, its dark-coloured back blends into the **gloom** of the ocean.

When a killer whale is seen from below, its white belly hides it against the bright surface of the water.

Survival skills

Because sharks have **gills**, they can hunt either at the surface or deep down in the ocean. Gills only work if water is flowing over them. If a shark stops swimming it will die.

gills

A killer whale's tail is so powerful it can keep its body out of the water while it looks around. A killer whale has lungs, not gills. It can hold its breath for up to 15 minutes.

Super senses

First a shark will hear a fish far away. As it gets closer it will smell it. Sharks have sensitive areas of skin that can feel tiny movements in the water. Last comes taste!

A killer whale makes clicking sounds that travel through the water and bounce off things nearby. By listening, the killer whale can work out how close its **prey** is.

Deadly weapons

A shark has a mouthful of fearsome teeth. If one of its teeth falls out, a new one grows back. A shark's skin is covered in tiny **scales**. They help the shark swim faster.

A killer whale's teeth are perfect for grabbing slippery, speedy **prey** like fish and seals. Its huge jaw **muscles** then keep a tight grip on struggling prey.

Hunting skills

Sharks live and hunt on their own. They are masters of the surprise attack. Sharks do not fight each other often, because they cannot hunt if they get hurt.

Killer whales live in family groups called pods. They are clever hunters. When one learns a new trick to catch **prey**, it can teach the skill to the rest of its pod!

Who wins?

What would happen if a shark faced a killer whale?

Sometimes these fights do happen. The killer whale would ram into the shark at top speed.

But who would win?

	Shark	Killer Whale
Size	6	10
Agility	9	7
Speed	7	9
Energy	10	7
Senses	10	8
Skin	8	8
Teeth	10	8
Armour	8	6
Hunting skills	8	10
Intelligence	6	10
TOTAL	82/100	**83/100**

KILLER WHALE WINS!

Picture glossary

fin part of a fish that helps it to swim

gill opening at the side of a fish's body which lets it breathe

gloom darkness or near-darkness

muscle a part of the body that causes movement

prey animals that are hunted and eaten by other animals

scales small overlapping plates that cover the skin of a fish or reptile

Find out more

Books

Hammerhead vs. Bull Shark (Who Would Win?), Jerry Pallotta (Scholastic, 2016)

Whales (Animal Lives), Sally Morgan (QED Publishing, 2014)

When Whales Cross the Sea (Extraordinary Migrations), Sharon Katz Cooper (Raintree, 2016)

Websites

www.discoverykids.com/category/sharks
Play fun games all about sharks.

www.killer-whale.org/killer-whale-facts
Find some top facts about killer whales.

www.ngkids.co.uk/animals/great-white-sharks
Ten facts about great white sharks, plus photos and a video to watch sharks in action.

Index